# MOVIE FAVORITES

### Solos and Band Arrangements
### Correlated with Essential Elements Band Method

### Arranged by
### MICHAEL SWEENEY

Welcome to Essential Elements Movie Favorites! There are two versions of each selection in this versatile book. The SOLO version appears on the left-hand page of your book. The FULL BAND arrangement appears on the right-hand page. Optional accompaniment recordings are available separately in CD or cassette format. Use these recordings when playing solos for friends and family.

ISBN 978-0-7935-5963-3

## HAL•LEONARD®
### CORPORATION
7777 W. BLUEMOUND RD. P.O. BOX 13819 MILWAUKEE, WI 53213

**From The Universal Motion Picture JURASSIC PARK**

# Theme From "Jurassic Park"

**BARITONE B.C.**
Solo

**Composed by JOHN WILLIAMS**
Arranged by MICHAEL SWEENEY

**MCA** music publishing

# Theme From "Jurassic Park"

**BARITONE B.C.**
**Band Arrangement**

**Composed by JOHN WILLIAMS**
Arranged by MICHAEL SWEENEY

**MCA** music publishing

00860019

**From CHARIOTS OF FIRE**
# CHARIOTS OF FIRE

BARITONE B.C.
Solo

Music by VANGELIS
Arranged by MICHAEL SWEENEY

00860019

# CHARIOTS OF FIRE

**BARITONE B.C.**
**Band Arrangement**

**Music by VANGELIS**
Arranged by MICHAEL SWEENEY

00860019

From THE MAN FROM SNOWY RIVER

# THE MAN FROM SNOWY RIVER

(Main Title Theme)

BARITONE B.C.
Solo

By BRUCE ROWLAND
Arranged by MICHAEL SWEENEY

# THE MAN FROM SNOWY RIVER

(Main Title Theme)

**BARITONE B.C.**
**Band Arrangement**

**By BRUCE ROWLAND**
Arranged by MICHAEL SWEENEY

**From The Paramount Motion Picture FORREST GUMP**

# FORREST GUMP - MAIN TITLE
## (Feather Theme)

BARITONE B.C.
Solo

**Music by ALAN SILVESTRI**
Arranged by MICHAEL SWEENEY

# FORREST GUMP - MAIN TITLE
## (Feather Theme)

BARITONE B.C.
**Band Arrangement**

Music by ALAN SILVESTRI
Arranged by MICHAEL SWEENEY

**From AN AMERICAN TAIL**

# SOMEWHERE OUT THERE

**BARITONE B.C.**
**Solo**

**Words and Music by JAMES HORNER,
BARRY MANN and CYNTHIA WEIL**
Arranged by MICHAEL SWEENEY

**MCA** music publishing

**From AN AMERICAN TAIL**

# SOMEWHERE OUT THERE

Words and Music by JAMES HORNER,
BARRY MANN and CYNTHIA WEIL
Arranged by MICHAEL SWEENEY

**BARITONE B.C.**
**Band Arrangement**

Moderately Slow

**MCA** music publishing

## From DANCES WITH WOLVES
# THE JOHN DUNBAR THEME

BARITONE B.C.
Solo

By JOHN BARRY
Arranged by MICHAEL SWEENEY

From DANCES WITH WOLVES
# THE JOHN DUNBAR THEME

**BARITONE B.C.**
**Band Arrangement**

By JOHN BARRY
Arranged by MICHAEL SWEENEY

00860019

**From The Paramount Motion Picture RAIDERS OF THE LOST ARK**

# RAIDERS MARCH

**By JOHN WILLIAMS**
Arranged by MICHAEL SWEENEY

**BARITONE B.C.**
**Solo**

RAIDERS MARCH

**BARITONE B.C.**
**Band Arrangement**

**By JOHN WILLIAMS**
Arranged by MICHAEL SWEENEY

**From Apollo 13**
# MUSIC FROM APOLLO 13
(End Credits)

**By JAMES HORNER**
Arranged by MICHAEL SWEENEY

**BARITONE B.C.**
Solo

**MCA** music publishing

# APOLLO 13

(End Credits)

**BARITONE B.C.**
**Band Arrangement**

By JAMES HORNER
Arranged by MICHAEL SWEENEY

MCA music publishing

00860019

From The Universal Picture E.T. (THE EXTRA-TERRESTRIAL)

# THEME FROM E.T. (THE EXTRA-TERRESTRIAL)

**BARITONE B.C.**
Solo

Music by JOHN WILLIAMS
Arranged by MICHAEL SWEENEY

MCA music publishing

# THEME FROM E.T. (THE EXTRA-TERRESTRIAL)

**BARITONE B.C.**
**Band Arrangement**

**Music by JOHN WILLIAMS**
Arranged by MICHAEL SWEENEY

00860019

**MCA** music publishing

# STAR TREK® THE MOTION PICTURE

**BARITONE B.C.**
Solo

**Music by JERRY GOLDSMITH**
Arranged by MICHAEL SWEENEY

# STAR TREK® THE MOTION PICTURE

**BARITONE B.C.**
**Band Arrangement**

**Music by JERRY GOLDSMITH**
Arranged by MICHAEL SWEENEY

00860019

# BACK TO THE FUTURE

**BARITONE B.C.**
Solo

By ALAN SILVESTRI
Arranged by MICHAEL SWEENEY

# BACK TO THE FUTURE

**BARITONE B.C.**
**Band Arrangement**

By ALAN SILVESTRI
Arranged by MICHAEL SWEENEY

00860019

MCA music publishing